COUNCIL *on*
FOREIGN
RELATIONS

Center for Preventive Action

I0026642

Discussion Paper Series on Managing Global Disorder No.1
June 2020

Perspectives on a Changing World Order

Paul B. Stares, Qingguo Jia, Nathalie Tocci,
Dhruva Jaishankar, and Andrey Kortunov

The Council on Foreign Relations (CFR) is an independent, nonpartisan membership organization, think tank, and publisher dedicated to being a resource for its members, government officials, business executives, journalists, educators and students, civic and religious leaders, and other interested citizens in order to help them better understand the world and the foreign policy choices facing the United States and other countries. Founded in 1921, CFR carries out its mission by maintaining a diverse membership, including special programs to promote interest and develop expertise in the next generation of foreign policy leaders; convening meetings at its headquarters in New York and in Washington, DC, and other cities where senior government officials, members of Congress, global leaders, and prominent thinkers come together with CFR members to discuss and debate major international issues; supporting a Studies Program that fosters independent research, enabling CFR scholars to produce articles, reports, and books and hold roundtables that analyze foreign policy issues and make concrete policy recommendations; publishing *Foreign Affairs*, the preeminent journal of international affairs and U.S. foreign policy; sponsoring Independent Task Forces that produce reports with both findings and policy prescriptions on the most important foreign policy topics; and providing up-to-date information and analysis about world events and American foreign policy on its website, CFR.org.

The Council on Foreign Relations takes no institutional positions on policy issues and has no affiliation with the U.S. government. All views expressed in its publications and on its website are the sole responsibility of the author or authors.

For further information about CFR or this paper, please write to the Council on Foreign Relations, 58 East 68th Street, New York, NY 10065, or call Communications at 212.434.9888. Visit CFR's website, CFR.org.

The Council on Foreign Relations acknowledges the Carnegie Corporation of New York for its generous support.

CONTENTS

INTRODUCTION

Paul B. Stares

Observers of world affairs like to point to a defining moment or pivotal event to proclaim the end of one era and the beginning of another. Not surprisingly, the novel coronavirus pandemic has already spawned much speculation that the world will undergo profound change as a consequence, even that contemporary history will forever be divided between what happened BC (before coronavirus) and AC (after coronavirus).[1] Historical eras, however, and certainly international orders—the complex amalgam of rules, norms, and institutions that govern relations among states at any given time—rarely, if ever, hinge on singular events. They, and the power relationships that undergird them, are simply too entrenched to change rapidly. For this reason, it is more accurate to identify transitional periods that span the rise and fall of specific international orders. In these periods, elements of the old order are still discernible, albeit functioning below their peak, while features of the new order are clearly emerging and playing a more influential role.[2]

Just such a situation appears to exist today. The international order largely constructed by the United States in the aftermath of World War II is still very much in evidence for the basic reason that most states appreciate its benefits and thus abide by its rules, all on the understanding that America retains sufficient power and influence to enforce compliance. At the same time, the global distribution of power is inexorably shifting with the rise of new powers as well as influential nonstate actors, such as multinational corporations and transnational terrorist organizations. The United States is also growing more reluctant to bear the costs of world leadership, especially when it comes to using military force. China and Russia, along with lesser regional powers, have taken advantage of this reticence in recent years to assert their own interests and to undermine the United States' international standing and authority. Their actions have at times openly flouted the rules and norms of the U.S.-led order without incurring a serious price, which has demoralized its supporters and emboldened its detractors.

In addition, the benefits of the U.S-led order and, in particular, the many international agreements that the United States has championed to open up the world to the free flow of goods, services, ideas, and people, no longer look so promising—not least to the many Americans whose livelihoods have suffered as a consequence. This shift has caused a public backlash against globalization not only in the United States but also in many Western countries that has manifested itself in more nationalist and inward-looking policies. As a result, the political will to defend, much less extend, the liberal international order is in short supply.

Where all this leads is by no means certain. It is still possible to imagine several alternative future orders arising from the current transitional period. One would be a world divided between states that subscribe to open market economies and democratic forms of governance and those that choose not to, likely led by the United States and China, respectively. Another would be an international system organized around rival trade blocs and associated political organizations, each dominated by the principal regional power. Both of these future orders could differ substantially, depending on whether relations between the constituent elements were essentially cooperative or highly competitive.

If previous transitional periods serve as any precedent, the actions of the major powers will likely determine which of these international orders—or a different one—emerges in the future. How the major powers have managed these consequential moments in the past is not encouraging, however. Since the beginning of the twentieth century, there have been three transitional periods: from approximately 1913 to 1920, from 1938 to 1947, and from 1988 to 1994. In two of these, catastrophic conflicts broke out (World Wars I and II), and the third experienced violent upheavals in the Balkans and the Middle East as well as in Africa and Asia. Efforts by major powers to create a robust, collective security arrangement in these transitional periods either collapsed or never lived up to their full promise (the League of Nations, the early "Four Policemen" proposal for the United Nations, and the vision of a "New World Order" after the 1991 Gulf War). Moreover, the international orders that followed—while bringing relative peace and stability—were flawed. Thus, the League of Nations system lacked the active involvement of the United States and the Soviet Union, the bipolar Cold War rested on the threat of mutual annihilation—and came close to it on several occasions—and the post–Cold War order revolved around the vagaries of U.S. hegemony.

Today, the signs are not promising that the major powers either comprehend the risks of the current transitional period or have a clear vision for a new international order that would be broadly acceptable and thus considered legitimate by most other states. If anything, mistrust and friction is steadily growing among them. The United States, China, India, and Russia are acquiring new strategic capabilities and exploiting new operational domains, specifically cyberspace and outer space, ostensibly to bolster deterrence and improve their national defenses. These preparations, however, can just as easily signal hostile intent and increase the scope for dangerous misunderstandings and unintended military escalation during acute crises. In short, the prospect of a war breaking out between two or more of the major powers, something that was generally considered to be risibly improbable just a few years ago, is no longer unimaginable.

Growing strategic rivalry among the major powers has also started to play out in many regions of the world as each increasingly maneuvers for influence and advantage. If the experience of the Cold War provides any guide, this competition could exacerbate local sources of instability and conflict. At the same time, the United Nations' ability to address, much less resolve, these and other threats to peace is declining as the organization becomes consumed by growing acrimony among the major powers and thus essentially as deadlocked as it was for most of the Cold War. Finally, cooperation on a host of critical global challenges and common security concerns—particularly nuclear proliferation, transnational terrorism, public health threats, and the interacting effects of climate change, resource scarcity, and environmental degradation—seems also likely to suffer. Those problems can be meaningfully tackled only through collective international action, which is unlikely to coalesce without impetus from the major powers. Despite a common interest in addressing those threats, increasing mistrust and antagonism will only make the task more difficult. The poor level of international cooperation on the COVID-19 outbreak—certainly in its initial stages—stands in stark contrast to what happened during the 2008–09 financial crisis and would appear to validate this fear.

It was with these concerns in mind that the Center for Preventive Action (CPA) at the Council on Foreign Relations launched the Managing Global Disorder project with the generous support of the Carnegie Corporation of New York. At the outset, CPA thought it valuable to get different perspectives on the state of the world from leading scholars in each of the major powers.[3] Each scholar was asked to address a common set of questions about the current international order—its current state, its likely future evolution, the risk of major war, and the prospects for cooperation on common security concerns and other global challenges. The answers, which were drafted before COVID-19, vary considerably, which is not surprising given their different vantage points.

Qingguo Jia from China argues that the post–World War II order is not ending but is clearly in "serious trouble" as a result of recent developments. Military conflict among the major powers, particularly between the United States and China, remains unlikely, however, given the shared incentives to avoid such a catastrophe. Their relationship will nevertheless grow more competitive. If the current international order is to be sustained for the benefit of all, the leading powers will need to work together to reform its working practices and institutions in a mutually satisfactory and sustainable way.

Nathalie Tocci from Italy is much less sanguine. She sees the liberal international order as "fraying" badly, and though the risk of war is not preordained, "potent drivers" are at work that make it more likely. The European Union (EU), she argues, needs to wake up to the evolving reality of growing rivalry among the major powers and develop a coherent and practical new strategy for defending EU interests and preserving the multilateral institutions of the current rules-based international order. The world will become more unstable and dangerous if the practice of multilateralism is replaced by narrow, nationalistic approaches.

Dhruva Jaishankar from India also views the world as in a transitional phase, but, unlike Jia and Tocci, sees it evolving in a more complex way with elements of unipolarity, bipolarity, and multipolarity coexisting uneasily. He shares Tocci's concern, however, that if current multilateral approaches to international problem-solving become "undermined, bypassed, or disregarded," then the risk of great power conflict will increase. The development of new and potentially threatening military capabilities, the trend toward economic "decoupling," and rising nationalism around the world are all concerning. To avoid the world growing more fragmented and dangerous, existing global governance institutions will need to adapt and new ones be created to accommodate rising powers.

Andrey Kortunov from Russia sees the world as entering a period of increasing volatility if the leading powers do not adjust to its new realities and new imperatives. In contrast to the other commentators, however, he sees the greater risk stemming less from great power competition and more from the uneven reach and benefits of globalization.

This is leaving many parts of the world further behind in terms of living standards and future prospects. Conflict in the future is more likely to occur, he believes, between states that are the winners and the losers of globalization—the haves and the have-nots—as well as within countries where the socioeconomic disparities are greatest. The major powers, he argues, should not only develop new crisis management mechanisms to lessen the ancillary risks of their growing rivalry but also work together to ensure that global institutions such as the United Nations, as well as various regional bodies, are able to manage these growing international schisms.

While each of these scholars views the world today and the challenges that lay ahead in different ways, they share a common belief that the opportunity to shape a new international order that is stable, inclusive, and beneficial to all still exists, though the window to do this is growing smaller. The experience of earlier transitional periods suggests that any effort to reform or create a new global order must be a collaborative undertaking. It cannot be imposed or established by any major power acting alone or even in concert with another. The same is true for managing the major challenges that humanity now confronts. Although the world seems destined to grow more competitive, congested, and contested in the coming years, the logic of major power cooperation is inescapable.

Such cooperation will be rendered more difficult, if not impossible, if the major powers grow increasingly fearful of each other's strategic intentions. Meaningful cooperation requires basic mutual trust and security, which will not arise spontaneously. The major powers will, therefore, need to provide active reassurance through formal agreement, where possible, and informally when this is not politically practical. The goal should be to create a stable and mutually beneficial understanding that accepts the reality of strategic competition as well as the imperative of coexistence. At a minimum, this objective will require a deeper appreciation of each country's core national security interests and a renewed commitment to the fundamental international principles of political sovereignty, domestic noninterference, and territorial integrity. In some areas, the major powers will also need to practice reciprocated restraint on activities deemed potentially threatening, as has been done in previous eras of major power competition.

The subsequent discussion papers in this series explore in greater depth how to promote a stable and mutually beneficial relationship among the major powers that can in turn provide the essential foundation for greater cooperation on pressing global and regional challenges.

CHINA

Qingguo Jia

Recent tensions in China-U.S. relations appear to support the claim that the post–World War II international order is coming to an end. In its place is a return to the great power rivalry and beggar-thy-neighbor competition that characterized the pre–World War I era. Careful analysis, however, shows that the postwar order is in no way over. Instead, it is evolving. Despite serious challenges and innate problems, it will persist as long as the great powers—and others—pursue necessary reforms to accommodate their respective interests while also taking care of those of others. All countries would benefit from sticking to the prevailing international order and making it work.

THE ORIGINS OF THE CURRENT INTERNATIONAL ORDER

Emerging from World War II as the preeminent world power, the United States was instrumental in creating a new international order, primarily because it realized that shaping the rules, norms, and institutions of the new era would protect its global interests. Maintaining world order is, however, a costly business. As Paul Kennedy describes in his book *The Rise and Fall of the Great Powers*, great powers decline not because rising powers defeat them but because the cost of maintaining world order drains their resources. To avoid or postpone this, the United States did three things in the wake of World War II: preserved and enhanced its wartime system of military alliances, established a UN-centered group of international institutions and mechanisms, and developed partnerships with other countries. Through these efforts, the United States effectively enlisted others to help maintain world order at minimal cost.

But ensuring that help entailed costs and constraints for the United States. These included providing and coordinating initiatives for international action; abiding by the rules and norms of various institutions, occasionally even at the expense of perceived U.S. interests; and dealing generously with allies and partners, including burden-sharing within alliance arrangements and allowing access to markets. At times, the costs have seemed excessive to American voters, leading to demands for more contributions from others. However, successive U.S. administrations, until that of Donald J. Trump, had decided that the benefits outweighed the costs and largely maintained the arrangement. In retrospect, the United States has benefited tremendously from such practices. Most telling, it has remained the preeminent global power for seven decades, despite the challenges of the Cold War and its aftermath.

THE ORDER IN CRISIS

This international order is now in serious trouble. The United States' willingness to maintain world order has significantly declined, particularly under the Trump administration. Although every previous U.S. president put U.S. interests first in foreign policy, the Trump administration has gone much further both in rhetoric and action—often at the expense of other countries and, in the long run, of the United States. Moreover, it has turned away from its leadership responsibilities in world affairs and even taken actions that have undermined existing international institutions, including withdrawing from the UN Educational, Scientific, and Cultural Organization (UNESCO), the Trans-Pacific Partnership, and the Paris Agreement on climate change. The Trump administration has also challenged World Trade Organization (WTO) rules by taking unilateral actions against other countries on trade disputes. Although this is not the first time the United States has pursued its interests at the expense of others or defied international institutions, the breadth and scope of the Trump administration's actions are categorically different. Given the pivotal role the United States plays in maintaining the world order, it can inflict significant damage and has done so.

The capacity of Western countries, which have been the strongest supporters of the current world order, to maintain that order has also declined sharply, especially since the end of the Cold War. Statistics show that the share of the world's gross domestic product of Group of Seven (G7) countries—the United States, Canada, France, Germany, Italy, Japan, and the United Kingdom—dropped from 68 percent in 1992 to 47 percent in 2015.[1] It dropped again to 30.15 percent in 2018 and is projected to go down to 27.26 percent in 2023.[2] Although the decline in military capabilities is more moderate, North Atlantic Treaty Organization (NATO) spending has also shrunk from two-thirds of global defense spending to little more than half in 2017.[3] On top of this, the Trump administration's America First policy has strained the unity of the West. Since the end of World War II, the West's ability to maintain the world order has never been weaker.

Other major countries have become increasingly dissatisfied and frustrated with existing international arrangements as well. Russia begrudges NATO expansion; India is unhappy with the perceived inadequate international recognition of its status as a great power; and China is frustrated that its voice and interests have not received due attention and respect. Those countries and others are seeking a change in the current international arrangement. China's efforts to assert its interests receive the most attention. As the leading rising power, China has created a number of initiatives to improve international cooperation, most notably through the Asian Infrastructure Investment Bank and the Belt and Road Initiative. These demands, given the sharply increased capabilities of the countries making them, have also strained the extant world order. For those and other reasons, the postwar world order is facing an unprecedented crisis.

PROBLEMS WITH THE EXISTING INTERNATIONAL ORDER

Some countries have lamented its decline, but the post–World War II order does have real problems. First, in the absence of effective checks against it, the United States has operated as the indispensable—and for many years undisputed—leader. This status has allowed it to abuse its power, at times even at the expense of its own interests as well as those of others, despite its professed good intentions. Washington has not always been prudent in conducting foreign policy, as evidenced by its decision to fight wars in Iraq and Vietnam, withdraw from international organizations, initiate trade wars despite WTO rules, and drag its feet in reforming international institutions. Power corrupts. This applies not only to domestic politics but also to international politics.

Second, the existing world order is excessively West-centric. Although Western countries do advocate certain worthy values, they do not have the right to dictate what other countries should do in their pursuit of political stability and economic development. Because every country faces a unique set of circumstances at home, the Western model does not always apply. That few developing countries have made it into the rank of developed countries over the past seven decades, despite the West's tremendous efforts—from a position of strength—to impose Western models, shows that this model has real problems in catering to the needs of developing countries.

Third, although the U.S.-led system of military alliances has been useful in helping maintain peace and stability, it is also exclusive and divisive. By default, it divides countries into allies and others. This approach has ensured alienation and suspicion on the part of the others and has provided a fertile ground for zero-sum interactions, making security cooperation difficult if not impossible.

Fourth, the existing economic order attaches considerable importance to efficiency, sacrificing equality. Under this order, the world has made great strides in liberalizing cross-border trade and investment, yielding an era of unprecedented prosperity. However, although a freer market has led to increased efficiency, it has also engendered greater inequality. Calls to address inequality are dismissed as calls for socialism and not taken seriously. Consequently, polarization is increasing both within and between countries, along with anti-globalization protests.

THE FUTURE OF WORLD ORDER

Despite its flaws, the current world order is still the best that humankind has created. Through established institutions, states champion universally accepted values and principles such as sovereignty, nonaggression, nonintervention in the internal affairs of other countries, human rights, rule of law, free trade, and the principle of common and differentiated responsibilities. States generally observe international laws and norms in light of the values and principles espoused by these institutions. Platforms have been created that offer countries an opportunity to air their frustrations with international arrangements and discuss ways and means to address pressing global issues. Another world war has thus far been avoided and unprecedented prosperity has been achieved. As a result, few countries have completely rejected the world order, regardless of any grudges they have against it.

Most nations have a stake in the existing order and are therefore more likely to stick with it. Wealthy countries expect that their wealth will be protected and poor countries expect aid when they are desperate. Both strong and weak states expect international laws and norms to protect their interests, one way or another. Most concerns are about perceived injustices in the distribution of benefits than about absolute losses. Some countries could be unhappy with a particular piece of an existing international arrangement but have no intention of overthrowing the world order as a whole in favor of a nineteenth-century arrangement (might is right). Thus, despite the U.S. withdrawal from some international institutions, most countries have chosen to stick with the existing order, whether by staying in institutions such as UNESCO and the Universal Postal Union or by observing the Joint Comprehensive Plan of Action and the Paris Agreement on climate change. Even rising powers such as China and India, which feel that the world order has not given their voices and interests adequate attention and respect, call for reform rather than replacement. For example, India wishes to be a permanent member of the UN Security Council and China hopes that its voting shares in the World Bank and International Monetary Fund will increase to reflect its growing economic clout.

Furthermore, although tensions between China and the United States are increasing, they will likely remain limited. Both are nuclear weapons states, both have stakes in the existing order despite unhappiness with aspects of it, and both are more or less interested in maintaining their shared economic relationship. Under these circumstances, neither fighting a war nor decoupling their economies is a realistic option. The relationship could become more competitive, but China and the United States have thus far continued to observe the Code for Unplanned Encounters at Sea in the South China Sea and to negotiate trade agreements, indicating that they know they should find a way to coexist. They are still cooperating on many issues, including pressuring North Korea to give up nuclear weapons, fighting international crimes, ensuring international aviation safety, and dealing with pandemic diseases such as COVID-19. Moreover, most other countries have a vested interest in a stable and constructive relationship between China and the United States and refuse to take sides.

Finally, given the United States' stake in the existing world order and that it can protect its interests only by maintaining that order, Washington will possibly have second thoughts about its current policies. After all, the Trump administration's policies thus far are an exception rather than the rule in post–World War II U.S. activities. A future administration could see things differently and adopt a watered-down version of traditional U.S. foreign policy.

The world order is evolving, but most established institutions and norms will likely remain. The United States will stay a leading power but could be less dominant. The West will continue to play a pivotal role but the world order will likely be less West-centric. When power is more diffuse, the world could be less efficient in addressing global challenges; at the same time, it could also adopt an approach that is more equal and consultative. The rising powers will likely have more power but also more responsibilities. Despite concerns about the decline of world order, countries can choose to transform it for the better.

To turn hope into reality, the major powers, especially China and the United States, should take up their respective responsibilities. They should resist the temptation to blame each other for the problems of existing institutions. Instead, they should carefully assess these institutions and identify areas that need improvement. They should consult with each other on that basis and jointly find a way to reform the extant international order in a way that accommodates their respective interests without undermining the interests of others. As the COVID-19 pandemic shows, the world is interconnected and mutually dependent. The only way to effectively deal with global issues is to embrace collaboration and cooperation. For a better future, cooperation is not a choice; it is a necessity.

THE EUROPEAN UNION

Nathalie Tocci

The liberal international order, within which the European project was established and is embedded, is fraying. This trend has been building up for more than a decade now. As Paul B. Stares argues, the world may have been living through a transitional period akin to those of 1913–20, 1938–47, and 1988–94. The novel coronavirus has exacerbated, accelerated, and increased everything from protectionism and great power rivalry to nationalism and ideological competition. As a result, the pandemic may represent the tipping point from the international liberal order to disorder. This reality should encourage Europeans to realize that rules-based multilateralism is not simply nice to have but essential, especially if they are to maintain their way of life in the years to come. No longer simply driven by the ideal of peace on the continent and the benefits of the single market, today the rationale for the European project is global. Nationalism—driven by nostalgia, the closure of borders, and racism—is being undermined by the creeping realization that size and clout matter more than ever. Only together can Europeans negotiate with China, stand up to Russia, rebuild bridges across the Atlantic, address global pandemics, govern migration, combat climate change, and embrace artificial intelligence and biotechnology while ensuring digital safety. Europeans have precious few alternatives to sticking together if they want a fair chance of thriving in the twenty-first century.[1] For precisely this reason, Europeans will perish in a world in which the strong (and big) do what they can while the weak (and small) suffer what they cannot avoid. Just as Europeans are bound to one another internally through the European Union (EU), the most radical form of multilateralism worldwide, they also have a stake in the broader world, in which multilateralism is a defining feature. This bestows on the EU a new and global raison d'être, one that poses a unique danger if the EU fails to rise to the challenge but that also holds great promise to reenergize the European project.

THE END OF THE LIBERAL INTERNATIONAL ORDER

Today's historical juncture offers few certainties. However, the post–World War II liberal international order has certainly ended. The so-called liberal international order rose from the ashes of two world wars. With it came the emergence and consolidation of the United Nations, the proliferation of international organizations, the slow but steady affirmation of international law, and the mushrooming of regional cooperation and integration initiatives, of which the European Union has been the most successful example. It first crystallized in the West during the Cold War and was extended after the fall of the Iron Curtain and the collapse of the Soviet Union. It was an order some reviled and others embraced.

Some mourn, others applaud, and others are not yet willing to accept the end of the liberal international order.[2] However, few if any would dispute that the distribution of power within the international system is changing dramatically. The distribution of power is complicated.[3] Its complexity is derived from concomitant trends: a traditional shift of power away from a global hegemon—the United States—toward multiple power centers and a diffusion of power, driven first by globalization and now by the fourth industrial revolution.[4] Power is not shifting simply from the West to the East but also beyond state boundaries, flowing across air, land, sea, space, and cyberspace.

The institutions, rules, and regimes built on the previous configuration of power—the liberal international order—will inevitably change to reflect this profound shake-up of the international system. This does not mean that all of its features, including its rules, regimes, and institutions, will disappear. Some will change, others will wane, and others will acquire renewed salience. In other words, the international order or disorder that follows will be non-liberal; shaped by liberal democracies and illiberal or authoritarian states, it will likely feature structured global cooperation on some issues like climate change, and transactional or ad hoc approaches to other issues like digital governance.

THE RISK OF GREAT POWER CONFLICT

Proponents of realism are quick to point out that, in a sinister repetition of history, the world, and in particular the United States and China, are sleepwalking into a Thucydides's trap—the theory that all rising powers inevitably clash with the predominant powers.[5] Although falling into the trap has never been preordained, the structural underpinnings of the power shift, coupled with misperception and miscommunication, have created potent drivers for conflict. This is not to say that history will repeat itself. However, the competition between the United States and China has morphed from commercial to technological rivalry and, during the COVID-19 crisis, has acquired ideological undertones. This competition could, in turn, result in a twenty-first-century military confrontation.

Liberal observers would be hard pressed to reach a fundamentally different conclusion as international institutions, rules, and regimes have been hollowed out and marginalized, or have collapsed outright. These weak or effectively moribund international institutions are no longer capable of creating a controlled setting for the peaceful management of conflict. Russia's violation of the Intermediate Range Nuclear Forces Treaty, which the United States met by withdrawing from the agreement, underscores both the fragility of institutional arrangements and how their unraveling heightens the risk of devastatingly violent conflict. Given that the United States is no longer willing and able to sustain an international order larger than itself and no other global actor is in a position to fully step into the void, the multilateral rules-based order is at risk. Multipolarity could eventually lead to strengthened multilateralism. But, in the slow and convulsed process of transition from a unipolar to a multi-, inter-, or nonpolar system, multilateralism is taking a hard hit, and, with it, the potential for the peaceful management of international relations has been reduced dramatically.

Constructivists, arguing that history is shaped not merely by objective, material forces, but by inter-subjectively defined identities and interests, are pessimistic as well. Because identities are constructed in mutually exclusive ways, the potential for violent conflict escalates. Whether one pits the West against Islam, liberal democracies against authoritarianism, cosmopolitans against nativists, or elites against the people, twenty-first-century constructs of identity have set the scene for violent conflict.

Some features of a twenty-first-century global confrontation can be discerned. From the Middle East to eastern Europe and from the Balkans to the Korean Peninsula, great power rivalry interlocks with and exacerbates regional power struggles, state fragility, and violent conflict. Other features, though arguably far more consequential—notably the links between economic and technological rivalry and the risk of military confrontation; the trade-offs between public health, political rights, and economic development; or the nexus between climate change and mass displacement—will be more difficult to predict.

ADDRESSING THE CHALLENGES: MULTILATERALISM AND THE EU'S ROLE

In this changing international environment, the EU has been imbued with a new sense of responsibility to sustain a rules-based multilateralism. Doing so requires both hard work and imagination. Part of the approach covers well-trodden ground. The EU should invest more in the UN system, both politically and financially, and spur reform of the World Trade Organization (WTO), notably its dispute settlement system, and of other international financial institutions to make them more representative and legitimate. The EU should also defend and implement international agreements and law, particularly by supporting the Joint Comprehensive Plan of Action with Iran. It should support forms of regional cooperation in Africa, Asia, and Latin America, which are the building blocks of global governance. It should also better coordinate internally, both between member states and across institutions and policy fields.

However, these actions will be insufficient on their own. The EU should also support multilateralism in at least three ways. First, it should systematically transform its bilateral or interregional arrangements into multilateral agreements. This means bringing the multilateral agenda forward in all of its bilateral and regional relationships, as well as making multilateral cooperation more central to EU activities, particularly in promoting sustainable development. For example, in order to better address youth and migration issues, the EU is already working to expand its bilateral relationship with the African Union into a trilateral partnership with the United Nations. Similarly, the EU could leverage its trade policy, which includes its relationships with Canada (through the Comprehensive and Economic Trade Agreement), Japan, members of Mercosur, Mexico, and others, to create a coalition to reform the stalled WTO.

Second, European foreign policy should acknowledge that a fixed set of like-minded countries to which it can automatically and lazily turn no longer exists. From like-minded partnerships, the EU should shift to like-minded partnering, in which the EU, guided by its principled goals, pragmatically identifies and fosters the appropriate multilateral group of actors on any given geographical or thematic issue. The constellation of actors will invariably change from issue to issue and, occasionally, within the same issue area as time (and governments) go by. The group of partners on the Iranian nuclear deal is not the same as for the conflict in Ukraine. The multilateral coalition in favor of a progressive climate agreement in Paris in 2015 was not the same as for a more ambitious outcome in Madrid four years later. Looking ahead, it remains to be seen whether the Group of Twenty (G20), which played a key role in the 2007–08 global financial crisis, will rise to the challenge of spurring post-COVID-19 economic recovery, or whether other multilateral formats will emerge instead. Principled and pragmatic partnering requires much more creativity in seeking out partners, a far greater capacity for listening to others, and more clarity and at times assertiveness on European interests and goals than was previously necessary.

Third, given the accelerated speed of politics in the digital age and the highly fluid nature of geopolitics, the EU should blend flexibility and inclusivity in its pursuit of effective multilateralism. This suggests the need for more frequent minilateral forums and contact groups to deliver multilateral results. The EU three (France, Germany, and Italy) format on the Iranian nuclear file and the International Contact Group on Venezuela are two examples. These are characterized by both an internal EU contact group (a subset of member states) and an international group of which the EU is a part. Such groups should be small enough to be agile and responsive but also large and varied enough to be representative. At the same time, to be legitimate, they should establish an institutional link to the larger multilateral setting, including both in internal EU features (connection between the European contact group and EU institutions) as well as in international settings (link between the international contact group and the United Nations).

The liberal international order is gone. But this does not mean that future generations will be relegated to a world of (seemingly) strong-men toying with the prospect of nuclear Armageddon as the planet is ravaged by climate change and technological progress races ahead, unchecked by shared norms and rules. A future international order could feature more challenges to norms and be less stable than the current international order. Yet it could also be more inclusive, more flexible, and ultimately more resilient.[6] The liberal international order may not survive, but what follows is not predetermined; it does not have to mean the end of the open, liberal values at the core of the European project. To maintain these values, Europeans and others should invest much more in multilateralism and, above all, be willing to break and recast the comfortable mold created in the recent past.

INDIA

Dhruva Jaishankar

The international order has changed radically over the past three decades in ways that are clearly discernible but not easily conceivable. This shift is evidenced by the lack of a commonly recognized term to characterize the emerging international order, beyond the increasingly inappropriate *post–Cold War*, which describes what the order is not. Without question, the prevailing international order has been under considerable strain, and the novel coronavirus has stretched it almost to a breaking point. Governance of the global commons is being undermined, rival economic institutions are being created, and international security institutions are increasingly anachronistic. The risk of great power conflict has increased as deterrence, interdependence, and socialization have given way to low-risk offensive weapons, changing cost-benefit calculations, and rising nationalism. Domestic political constraints in the United States, the nature of China's rise, and the role of other actors (Europe, India, Japan, and Russia) mean that the emerging international system could quite possibly reflect elements of unipolarity, bipolarity, and multipolarity simultaneously.

China and India are often grouped together as the two rising powers in Asia, but their interests and objectives differ. India desires a multipolar world in which it can protect its interests and play a role in shaping the international order. It also seeks stronger multilateral mechanisms to better manage the instability that will inevitably result from multipolarity. As a result, India rather paradoxically finds itself as a rising but largely status quo–oriented power, one that seeks to reform the international order but not necessarily overturn it. By contrast, China seeks to both reform and overturn many aspects of the international order. Consequently, China and India often find themselves working together to improve representation at international organizations and create parallel structures even as they seek different substantive outcomes on such issues as freedom of navigation and overflight, internet governance, and the sustainable financing of infrastructure.

The emerging international order will likely include elements of a unipolar, bipolar, and multipolar world, states competing for influence across domains and regions—even as they work through international institutions and regional coalitions. At the same time, questions about the future international order will revolve primarily around the relative power and orientation of the United States and China. A multipolar world is less stable than the alternatives. It involves more actors, and one actor shifting could upset the overall balance of power. However, for India, multipolarity would provide a way to secure its national interests without deferring to either the United States or China.

CHALLENGES FOR THE FUTURE INTERNATIONAL ORDER

The international order can be parsed into three elements. The first is the governance of the global commons, or domains outside the control of any single sovereign state. This extends to the management of international waters, the atmosphere, outer space, polar regions, and—by some definitions—cyberspace. The second is the governance of economic and trade exchanges between states. This could include multilateral lending, trade, immigration, regulations and standards, infrastructure financing, energy security, and international financial management. The third (and oldest) element of international order is the management of peace and security, including through arms control, international legal conventions, confidence-building measures, information exchanges, and military alliances and partnerships.

Achieving these objectives—governing the global commons, facilitating economic exchanges, and managing international security—has required numerous agreements, treaties, conventions, and international institutions. For example, managing the global commons required the UN Convention on the Law of the Sea (UNCLOS), the Paris Agreement, the Antarctic Treaty System, and the Outer Space Treaty. The World Trade Organization (WTO), the World Bank, the International Monetary Fund (IMF), the International Organization for Standardization, the Group of Twenty (G20), and many other such institutions support the international economic order. The security order has been based on the UN Security Council, Nuclear Nonproliferation Treaty (NPT), and alliances such as the North Atlantic Treaty Organization (NATO), among a multitude of bilateral, regional, and international agreements.

Of these three concepts, global governance has evolved the most since the end of the Cold War. UNCLOS has been imposed, an international climate change agreement has been finalized, and other such institutions have been strengthened. However, these agreements are under increasing stress, including from the world's second most powerful country, China. China has claimed territory in the South China Sea, tested anti-satellite systems at high altitudes, developed potential dual-use facilities in Antarctica, and created the Great Firewall to limit internet access. Of course, the United States has not helped matters either, failing to ratify UNCLOS and withdrawing from the Paris Agreement on climate change.

In speed and scale, China's rise and, to a lesser degree, India's, is without precedent. In U.S. dollars, the proportion of gross domestic product (GDP) between the United States, the big three European economies (France, Germany, and the United Kingdom), Japan, India, and China in 2000 was roughly 20–10–10–1–3. By 2018, it was 8–4–2–1–5. If the change between 2008 and 2018 is sustained for another decade, by 2028 it would be roughly 4–2–1–1–6. A great leveling of global economic power—if not diplomatic and military strength—is underway.

The international economic order faces obstacles, most notably stagnation at the WTO, both the Doha Development Round of negotiations and the hollowing out of dispute-resolution mechanisms. Moreover, in the absence of reform of the Bretton Woods institutions, China, India, and others have begun to create parallel structures. These include the Asian Infrastructure Investment Bank (AIIB) and the New Development Bank, which was created by Brazil, Russia, India, China, and South Africa (BRICS). The G20 parallels the Group of Seven, which once represented the world's seven largest economies. The international economic architecture is evolving to reflect the changing balance of power.

The greatest stagnation, however, concerns the international security order. Most associated institutions—from the UN Security Council and NPT to NATO—are relics of the Cold War. They reflect the priorities and power differentials of the 1940s or 1960s, and make decreasing sense today. The transition from the Cold War to the post–Cold War period was unusual in that it occurred without a major international conflict, which, though desirable, also limited opportunities to reset the international security order. More than any other area, the international security order of today is anachronistic. It can no longer dampen security competition, particularly in the Indo-Pacific and Middle East.

THE RISK OF GREAT POWER CONFLICT

The risk of great power conflict increases in a multipolar world in which multilateralism is undermined, bypassed, or disregarded. Optimists could argue that the absence of overt great power conflict in the Cold War and immediate post–Cold War periods was made possible by the presence of nuclear deterrents, economic interdependence facilitated by globalization, and greater socialization and acculturation. In terms that international relations theorists understand, these broadly reflect realist, liberal, and constructivist explanations.

However, reasons to doubt the continuing validity of each of these factors in preserving peace between the great powers are sound. First, new technologies risk overturning the offense-defense balance to which the world has become accustomed. Shortened decision-making times enabled by artificial intelligence and hypersonic weapons are already being combined with low-risk offensive capabilities enabled by cyber technologies and robotic warfare. Second, the limits of the pacifying effects of economic integration are already being exposed. Russia was willing to suffer major economic losses, including from energy exports to Europe, to annex Crimea. Pakistan has continued to perpetrate low-level conflict against India despite suffering mightily in economic terms. Third, a documented rise of nationalism in many major power countries risks reversing the integration and interdependence of states and the priorities of national leaderships. These trends, coupled with emerging multipolarity and an anachronistic security order, suggest the risk of great power conflict is higher than it has been since the end of World War II.

In sum, India is likely to face considerable adversity as it continues its rise. The notion of international order confronts major obstacles: an erosion of the governance of the global commons, competing economic structures, and vestigial security institutions. The drivers of great power competition, including low-risk and potent offensive weaponry, shifting cost-benefit considerations, and growing nationalism, are gradually supplanting drivers of great power cooperation—nuclear deterrence, economic interdependence, and social exchanges. India cannot afford to be marginalized. Thus, even as India will seek a multipolar order—one in which it has a seat and a say at the global high table—it will also seek stronger multilateral arrangements to mitigate competition and instability.

ADDRESSING THE CHALLENGE

To successfully prevent and mitigate future conflict, other major powers will need to understand the compulsions driving China and India, the largest rising powers that express both common and divergent approaches to the international order. To better represent the changing balance of power, China and India each desire to increase their stakes in existing multilateral institutions. In the absence of such reform, they have cooperated to establish parallel institutional structures. Thus, they work together on climate negotiations, including at the Copenhagen Summit, within BRICS, at the AIIB, and on certain issues, such as the responsibility to protect, at the United Nations.

At the same time, China and India seek different outcomes on many issues. India's tepid support for a multilateral approach to internet governance, its more vocal backing for freedom of navigation and overflight, and its obdurate boycott of the Belt and Road Initiative on normative grounds signal a sharpening of differences with China. These differences arise in part because India is a democratic polity and China is not; their approaches to global governance are an outgrowth of their contrasting approaches to domestic governance. India has positioned itself as a status quo power. China is perceived as revisionist. These differences have roots in how both states were established: India became independent in a nonviolent struggle and the People's Republic of China was established as the culmination of a revolutionary movement. These factors perhaps explain why many observers tend to either conflate China and India, and in the process overlook the sharpening differences in behavior and outlook, or contrast the two, but express surprise about their cooperation at international institutions.

Managing this apparent paradox will require the established powers—the United States, Europe, and, on some issues, Japan, Russia, and even China—to make room for others while defending and upholding the norms that have served the international system so well since the end of the Cold War. However, established powers are unlikely to be comfortable with this approach given that they are naturally mistrustful of the behavior of rising powers and seek to protect their privileges and securities. As a result, the prospect of UN Security Council, IMF, NPT, or Asian Development Bank reforms remains remote.

The best that can be hoped for under these circumstances is for India and like-minded states to better manage the impulses of revisionist great powers. A few principles, if adhered to, would help manage such revisionism. First, these states should establish rules of reciprocity so that authoritarian states cannot take advantage of democratic openness without opening themselves up further. This could extend, for example, to investment regimes, openness to media, intellectual property, and educational and research and development cooperation. Second, these states should place a premium on economic sustainability and the mutual benefits of growth, which in turn will require restructuring trade and technology arrangements. Today, the role of sovereign states has created a distortive effect in market economies. A more level economic playing field will be necessary to sustain the economic dimensions of the international order. Third, these states should invest in military preparedness, particularly military technologies that can play a defensive or denial role, to resist territorial revisionism and mitigate competition. As part of this effort, these states should also initiate a new round of arms control arrangements to address a host of lethal emerging technologies. Overall, India and other like-minded states should manage a multipolar world by establishing and enforcing multilateral agreements to foster new norms and thereby revitalize, not replace, the international order.

RUSSIA

Andrey Kortunov

Two distinct but overlapping international agendas shape the complex global environment. The first reflects the concerns of the twentieth and early twenty-first centuries; the second reflects new and emerging threats. The old world agenda is disintegrating quickly and the new one is yet to be set. As a result, the world has entered a period of increasing instability, volatility, and uncertainty. To minimize the risk of armed conflict and to shape the new agenda, major powers, regional organizations, and international institutions should focus on developing confidence-building measures in technical or regionally specific areas, such as arms control agreements, to build consensus and create acceptable dispute-resolution mechanisms. As consensus builds, new voluntary agreements on emerging challenges and on international rules, norms, and regimes should be developed. In this way, major powers and rising powers can work together to manage the risk of armed conflict and create a more inclusive system of global governance.

THE FUTURE OF WORLD ORDER

Globalization has shaped world affairs for many decades, but the dynamics of the globalization process have turned out more complicated and less linear than many experts anticipated in the late 1980s and early 1990s. It was assumed then that waves of globalization would spread mainly from the economic, political, and technological "core" of the Western world to the "periphery," or the residual rest. Large "semi-peripheral" countries—such as Brazil, China, India, Russia, and others—would become transmission mechanisms linking the "global core" to the "global periphery." Consequently, experts predicted that countries moving closer to the core (or, to the West) would embrace globalization, while resistance to globalization would increase as countries moved toward the periphery. These peripheral countries would also be more nationalistic and isolationist, and more likely to generate trade wars and conflict.

However, events of the early twenty-first century suggest that, in many cases, the waves of globalization are moving in the opposite direction—from the global periphery to the global core. Rather than push for global interconnectedness, the West is trying to fence itself off from the periphery by implementing restrictions on migration, adopting protectionist policies, repatriating previously abandoned industries, and allowing the rise of nationalism. Although Western countries as a whole currently surpass non-Western countries in their involvement in the globalization process, the question of who will become the main driver of this process in the future remains open. The core could ultimately be less globalized than the periphery.

Turning back or even significantly slowing down globalization in the foreseeable future is not possible. Even the COVID-19 pandemic, which has imposed rigid restrictions on some specific avenues of globalization, including international travel, has at the same time opened new routes for bringing humankind together by, for example, boosting international online job opportunities. Among other things, the pandemic has graphically illustrated that the world is getting smaller, more crowded, more complex, and more fragile. In the aftermath of the immediate repercussions of COVID-19, the world and its constituent parts are likely to become more, rather than less, interconnected and interdependent. Once the global economy has overcome the current recession, transnational flows of finances, goods and services, ideas, and people will start growing again, pressures from common problems will likely increase, and the need to upgrade the current system of global governance will become increasingly urgent.

The process of globalization will remain fundamentally uneven, however, in terms of who benefits the most and how it affects culture, the economy, and society. Large parts of the world will likely remain excluded for a long time—not only failing states, but also regions within successful states that lag behind or fail. Some countries with strong economic sectors will be leaders in globalization; others will likely continue to oppose it. The dynamics of the global financial market will outpace the dynamics of the global labor market; globalization of science will progress faster than the globalization of culture.

As a result, the primary battle of the future will not be a competition between a small group of major global actors, nor a competition between a broader group of states—although a devolution of power in the international system will likely continue. The great divide in international relations will be between the winners and losers of the globalization process, those countries that can best adapt to an increasingly dynamic and less certain global environment. This divide already cuts across existing coalitions, blocs, continents, individual countries, and even cities; it will make the transition to a new system of global governance painful and protracted. Consequently, a period of instability, multiple crises, and political volatility at the national, regional, and global levels could last for several decades.

MANAGING THE RISK OF WAR BETWEEN GREAT POWERS

The process of globalization should gradually shift the focus of the international system away from traditional great power competition to tensions between the global core and the global periphery. Large-scale military conflicts within the core are unlikely. In 1914, leaders of great powers had efficient instruments for mobilizing their societies to fight a large-scale war in the middle of Europe. Today, such mobilization looks impossible, even in authoritarian countries such as China or Russia. Moreover, control over territory, natural resources, or even over trade routes is no longer as critical to great powers as it was one or two hundred years ago.

However, the risk of a direct military confrontation between major powers will by no means disappear. At least two sets of circumstances could lead to such a confrontation. First, a technical or human error, a mistaken assessment of an opponent's intentions, or an inadvertent escalation of a political crisis could trigger a conflict between major powers. To reduce the risk of triggering these circumstances, great powers should maintain open lines of political communication and participate in a broad range of confidence-building measures and various forms of military-to-military collaboration, among other steps. New formats for strategic arms control will emerge.

Second, a direct military confrontation could result from intense regional crises fought by proxies or from civil conflicts in places regarded as top security priorities by a great power, or several great powers (such as Ukraine for Russia, Venezuela or Israel for the United States, or Taiwan for China). Here again, the importance of direct political communication and military-to-military communication on the ground—as Russia and the United States do in Syria—is evident. Future states may not recognize the concept of spheres of influence but will have to accept implicitly the notion of spheres of special sensitivity for the major powers. This acceptance could decrease the risk of a direct military collision between major powers.

ADDRESSING COMMON SECURITY CHALLENGES

Over time, the scale and the number of common security challenges will grow, as will public demands to turn these challenges into top foreign policy priorities for major powers. These challenges will increasingly compete with more traditional foreign policy agendas, including the remnants of great power competition. As a result, major powers will need to pursue parallel foreign policy tracks: the old track, inherited from the twentieth and the beginning of the twenty-first centuries; and the new track, reflecting emerging international realities of the twenty-first century.

Ideally, these tracks should be kept separate—similar to U.S. policies during the Cold War, when strategic arms control policies with the Soviet Union were insulated from the rest of the relationship between the two superpowers. However, complete separation is not achievable: the nature of the new challenges will require a certain trust among major powers. The United States and the Soviet Union achieved only minimal trust during the Cold War, but that did allow them to sign historic arms control agreements. In applying this concept to conflicts today, major powers are unlikely to participate in any strategic interaction to fight international terrorism if they are also operating within the framework of a predominantly adversarial major power relationship.

Merging the needs of a new foreign policy track with the limitations derived from the old track will likely be one of the main obstacles to enhancing global and regional governance. Nevertheless, the new track should gradually gain priority. The new rules of engagement and the new models of interaction will grow from technical, specific, and incremental pockets of cooperation, and eventually expand to more sensitive political and strategic domains. The new track will likely produce fewer old-fashioned, legally binding agreements and new international institutions. Instead, states will accede to voluntary regimens, unilateral commitments, and public-private partnerships.

MANAGING REGIONAL DISORDER

Regional crises and conflicts will continue, mostly along the borders between the global core and the global periphery. The Middle East and North Africa will likely remain the most significant global generators of instability, but other explosive regions, such as sub-Saharan Africa and South Asia, are also likely loci of violent outbursts. Crises will stem from failures of regional economic and social development strategies; they will be aggravated by the continued growth of international radical networks, global problems such as climate change, and major power competition.

Given the diversity of regional conflicts, a standardized approach to mitigating or containing them is difficult to envision. In some relatively uncontroversial cases (Yemen), the United Nations could play the leading role in the quest for settlements. In other cases (India-Pakistan), the parties to the conflict are more likely to support direct interaction between the competing sides by encouraging cease-fires, confidence-building measures, and diplomatic compromises. Yet in other cases (Libya), external powers will likely focus on limiting the horizontal or vertical escalation of conflict situations.

An important dimension of conflict management will be conflict prevention. Its efficiency will depend to a large extent on the ability to link security and development needs in explosive parts of the world, to enhance the efficiency of technical assistance programs, and to develop the capacity of interested parties to react in a timely manner to natural and man-made disasters affecting fragile and failed states. At the same time, states will need to master the ability to regulate transborder migration flows and the global arms trade, and to curb the proliferation of international terrorism.

Practical alternatives to the United Nations are hard to imagine in the near future. Prospects for a less divided and more functional United Nations are similarly unrealistic. UN reform will continue to be an uphill battle as long as fundamental differences exist between major powers regarding the likely and desirable new global order. Consequently, the role of the United Nations in critical matters (strategic arms control, nonproliferation, and many regional crises) will continue to be limited, and major powers will continue to violate the UN Charter.

At the same time, the United Nations can play a more active role in shaping the new international agenda, including by establishing rules of engagement for new challenges and threats. Major power competition has not yet entered new domains of world politics (such as cyberspace), which could create opportunities for the United Nations, especially if it operates in cooperation with other international institutions, such as the Asia-Pacific Economic Cooperation, BRICS (Brazil, Russia, India, China, and South Africa), the European Union, the Group of Seven, and the Group of Twenty.

Ideally, the global security role of the United Nations should be complemented at the regional level by appropriate collective security organizations, which should receive a UN mandate for managing crises and instabilities in their respective regions. These organizations should have the legitimacy, resources, and institutional capacities to provide for peace and security at the regional level. However, in areas of particular concern (East Asia, Europe, and the Middle East), such an arrangement will likely be beyond reach for a long time. Therefore, the immediate goal should not be to unite divided regions but rather to manage existing divisions to bring down risks (Russia and the West in Europe, China and the United States in East Asia, Iran and the Sunni monarchies in the Gulf). Over time, management of regional confrontations could lead to reconciliation and, eventually, to the establishment of a regional collective security system.

The transition to a new international system will be long and quite dangerous. It will involve a period of increased instability, volatility, and uncertainty as nation-states—and other global actors—seek to impose order and maintain or gain advantages. As a result, risk management and cost reduction should be urgent priorities for major powers. Perhaps most important, however, these powers should focus on making a compelling case for enhancements and improvements to global governance. Future governance structures should incorporate elements of the old order but prioritize reconciling the needs of rising powers and emerging threats of the twenty-first century.

Perspectives on a Changing World Order

ENDNOTES

INTRODUCTION

1. See, for example, Rana Foroohar, "Life BC and AC," *Financial Times*, March 23, 2020, http://ft.com/content/b83cb83f-4f72-4b31-aff0-2d398a8aa0ef; Mira Rapp-Hooper, "China, America, and the International Order After the Pandemic," *War on the Rocks*, March 24, 2020, http://warontherocks.com/2020/03/china-america-and-the-international -order-after-the-pandemic; and Thomas Wright, "Stretching the International Order to Its Breaking Point," *Order From Chaos* (blog), April 6, 2020, http://brookings .edu/blog/order-from-chaos/2020/04/06/stretching-the-international-order-to-its -breaking-point.

2. They can also be termed interregnums after the Italian sociologist Antonio Gramsci and his oft-quoted observation that "the crisis consists precisely in the fact that the old is dying and the new cannot be born; in this interregnum a great variety of morbid symptoms appear." See Antonio Gramsci, *Selections From the Prison Notebooks*, edited and translated by Quintin Hoare and Geoffrey Nowell Smith (London: Lawrence and Wishart, 1971), 276.

3. For this project, the major powers were limited to China, India, Russia, and the European Union (EU), recognizing that the EU is a supranational institution that aspires to act collectively on the world stage. Each can claim major power status for having two or more of the following characteristics: they are geographically large, have sizable populations, have nuclear weapons with intercontinental reach, have permanent representation in the UN Security Council, and are among the world's leading economies.

CHINA

1. Barry P. Bosworth, "Not-So-Great Expectations: The G-7's Waning Role in Global Economic Governance," *Order From Chaos* (blog), May 24, 2016, http://brookings.edu /blog/order-from-chaos/2016/05/24/not-so-great-expectations-the-g-7s-waning-role -in-global-economic-governance.

2. "Share of Global Gross Domestic Product from G7 and G20 Countries in 2019 and Projections for 2024," Statista, http://statista.com/statistics/722962/g20-share-of-global-gdp.

3. Andrew Macdonald, Fenella McGerty, and Guy Eastman, "NATO Members Drive Fastest Increase in Global Defense Spending for a Decade," IHS Markit, December 18, 2018, http://ihsmarkit.com/research-analysis/nato-members-drive-fastest-increase-in-global-defence-spending.html.

THE EUROPEAN UNION

1. Nathalie Tocci, "Navigating Complexity: The EU's Rationale in the 21st Century," Istituto Affari Internazionali, January 2019, http://iai.it/it/pubblicazioni/navigating-complexity-eus-rationale-21st-century.

2. See Richard N. Haass, "Liberal World Order, R.I.P.," Project Syndicate, March 21, 2018, http://project-syndicate.org/commentary/end-of-liberal-world-order-by-richard-n--haass; Sergei Karaganov and Dimitri Suslov, "A New World Order: A View From Russia," October 4, 2018, http://eng.globalaffairs.ru/articles/a-new-world-order-a-view-from-russia; and Robert Kagan, *The Jungle Grows Back: America and Our Imperiled War* (New York: Penguin Random House, 2018).

3. For an elaboration of this argument, see Nathalie Tocci, "The Demise of the International Liberal Order and the Future of the European Project," Istituto Affari Internazionali, November 19, 2018, http://iai.it/en/pubblicazioni/demise-international-liberal-order-and-future-european-project.

4. The fourth industrial revolution refers to the manner in which new technologies, notably in artificial intelligence and biotechnology, are fusing the biological, digital, and physical worlds, dramatically affecting economies, societies, and, arguably, human life itself.

5. Graham Allison, *Destined for War: Can America and China Escape Thucydides' Trap?* (New York: Houghton Mifflin Harcourt, 2017).

6. Tocci, "The Demise."

ACKNOWLEDGMENTS

Many deserve thanks for their work on this publication. To the authors who assessed the global challenges facing nation-states in the twenty-first century—and suggested clear ways to address these challenges—your insights should encourage major powers to recognize the importance of cooperation and conflict prevention.

This publication would not have been possible without the support and guidance of the Council on Foreign Relations' James M. Lindsay, senior vice president, director of studies, and Maurice R. Greenberg chair; and Shannon K. O'Neil, vice president, deputy director of studies, and Nelson and David Rockefeller senior fellow for Latin America Studies. My thanks also to Patricia Dorff, editorial director, and her team of editors: Chloe Moffett, Sumit Poudyal, and Katherine De Chant. Finally, my thanks to Jennifer Wilson, Megan Geckle, Ellie Estreich, and James West for their help in pulling this publication together.

We are also grateful for the generous support of the Carnegie Corporation of New York, without which this series of discussion papers and associated international workshops would not have been possible.

Paul B. Stares
June 2020

ABOUT THE AUTHORS

Paul B. Stares is the General John W. Vessey senior fellow for conflict prevention and director of the Center for Preventive Action at the Council on Foreign Relations (CFR). Prior to joining CFR, Stares was vice president and director of the Center for Conflict Analysis and Prevention at the U.S. Institute of Peace. An expert on conflict prevention and a regular commentator on current affairs, he is the author or editor of nine books on U.S. security policy and international relations. His latest book, *Preventive Engagement: How America Can Avoid War, Stay Strong, and Keep the Peace*, provides a comprehensive blueprint for how the United States can manage a more turbulent and dangerous world. Stares has participated in various high-level studies, including the Genocide Prevention Task Force, co-chaired by Madeleine Albright and William Cohen; the expert working group on the strategic environment for the Iraq Study Group, co-chaired by James Baker and Lee Hamilton; and the Task Force on Extremism in Fragile States, co-chaired by Thomas Kean and Lee Hamilton. He received his BA from North Staffordshire Polytechnic and both his MA and PhD from Lancaster University.

Qingguo Jia is dean of the School of International Studies at Peking University. He is a member of the Standing Committee and the Foreign Affairs Committee of the National Committee of the Chinese People's Political Consultative Conference. He is also the director of the Institute for China-U.S. People-to-People Exchange of the Ministry of Education, vice president of the Chinese American Studies Association, vice president of the China International Relations Studies Association, and vice president of the Chinese-Japanese Studies Association. Jia also serves on the editorial board of more than a dozen established domestic and international academic journals. He has taught at the

University of Vermont; Cornell University; University of California, San Diego; University of Sydney in Australia; and Peking University. Previously, he was a Center for Northeast Asian Policy Studies fellow at the Brookings Institution from 2001 to 2002, a visiting professor at the University of Vienna in 1997, and a research fellow at the Brookings Institution from 1985 and 1986. He has published extensively on U.S.-China relations, relations between the Chinese mainland and Taiwan, Chinese foreign policy, and Chinese politics. He received his PhD from Cornell University.

Nathalie Tocci is director of the Istituto Affari Internazionali and honorary professor at the University of Tübingen. She recently served as special advisor to the EU's high representative for foreign affairs and security policy, on behalf of whom she wrote and worked on the implementation of the European global strategy. Previously, Tocci held research positions at the Centre for European Policy Studies in Brussels; the Transatlantic Academy in Washington, DC; and the Robert Schuman Centre for Advanced Studies in Florence. Her most recent publications include *Framing the EU's Global Strategy and the EU*, *Promoting Regional Integration*, and *Conflict Resolution*. Tocci is the 2008 winner of the Anna Lindh award for the study of European foreign policy. She received her BA from University College at Oxford and both her MA and PhD from the London School of Economics and Political Science.

Dhruva Jaishankar is director of the U.S. Initiative at the Observer Research Foundation. He is also a nonresident fellow with the Lowy Institute in Australia and a columnist for the *Hindustan Times*. Jaishankar was previously a fellow at Brookings India, Brookings Institution, and the German Marshall Fund, where he managed the India Trilateral Forum—a regular policy dialogue involving participants from India, Europe, and the United States. He was also a visiting fellow at the S. Rajaratnam School of International Studies at Nanyang Technological University in Singapore. He has a BA from Macalester College and an MA from Georgetown University.

Andrey Kortunov has been director general of the Russian International Affairs Council since 2011. He is a member of expert and supervisory committees and boards of trustees of several Russian and international organizations. Previously, Kortunov taught at the University of California, Berkeley, among other universities, and led several public organizations involved in higher education, social sciences, and social development. From 1982 to 1995, he held various positions at the Institute for U.S. and Canada Studies, including as deputy director. Kortunov received his PhD from the Moscow State Institute of International Relations.

ABOUT THE CENTER
FOR PREVENTIVE ACTION

The Center for Preventive Action (CPA) seeks to help prevent, defuse, or resolve deadly conflicts around the world and to expand the body of knowledge on conflict prevention. It does so by creating a forum in which representatives of governments, international organizations, nongovernmental organizations, corporations, and civil society can gather to develop operational and timely strategies for promoting peace in specific conflict situations. The center focuses on conflicts in countries or regions that affect U.S. interests, but may be otherwise overlooked; where prevention appears possible; and when the resources of the Council on Foreign Relations can make a difference. The center does this by

- issuing regular reports to evaluate and respond rapidly to developing sources of instability and formulate timely, concrete policy recommendations that the U.S. government, international community, and local actors can use to limit the potential for deadly violence;

- engaging the U.S. government and news media in conflict prevention efforts. CPA staff members meet with administration officials and members of Congress to brief on CPA's findings and recommendations, facilitate contacts between U.S. officials and important local and external actors, and raise awareness among journalists of potential flashpoints around the globe;

- building networks with international organizations and institutions to complement and leverage the Council's established influence in the U.S. policy arena and increase the impact of CPA's recommendations; and

- providing a source of expertise on conflict prevention to include research, case studies, and lessons learned from past conflicts that policymakers and private citizens can use to prevent or mitigate future deadly conflicts.